THE POWER OF THE RESURRECTION

Alvin Russell White Jr

Copyright © 2022 by Alvin Russell White Jr

All rights reserved.

Contents

Introduction: The Power Of The Resurrection v

Chapter One: The Reason for The Resurrection 1
Chapter two: The Power to change 10
Chapter three: The Power to Forgive 16
Chapter four: The Power to Witness 21
Chapter Five: The Power of The Comforter 28
Chapter six: The Keeping Power of the Resurrection 32
Chapter Seven: The Power of Intercession 35
Chapter Eight: The Power of the Resurrection 40
Chapter Nine: The Hope of the Resurrection 45

Reference list 52
Scripture Reference List 53
Song Reference List 55

Introduction:

THE POWER OF THE RESURRECTION

The Christian life rests its power on the power of the resurrection. The apostle Paul said in his letter to the church in Philippi, "That I may know Him, and the power of His resurrection." Philippians 3:10. We see that Paul knew the importance of the power of the resurrection, however, Paul longed to know more of its Power.

What do we know about the resurrection? What do we know about its power? I want to know more of the power of the resurrection. Christians should know the reasons for the resurrection. Christians should find the power of the resurrection working in their lives. Like the apostle Paul, we too should have a desire to know Him more deeply. We should want to see the power working in us, as it did in the life of Paul.

So, let us begin to open God's word and see where it will lead us. What will we find? With open hearts will we obey? My prayer is that we all may know Him and the power of His resurrection.

Chapter One: The Reason for The Resurrection

Why was the resurrection necessary? Why did Christ have to die? What is the reason for redemption? We will need to explore the answers to these questions as we investigate the power of the resurrection, and what it means to us today.

When we look at the reasons for the Resurrection, we will look at the very beginning, the creation of the universe. In Genesis chapter one it tells us how God created the sun, moon, stars, land, trees, flowers, and animals, and all other things. The best of God's creation was mankind. Mankind was made in the image of God and was given a living soul. Look how Genesis tells it.

"So, God Created man in His own image, in the image of God created He him; male and female created He them." Genesis 1:27.

God took special care of mankind and placed him in a garden. Mankind, however, was not made lawless. Genesis says,

"And the LORD God took the man and put him into the garden of Eden to dress it and to keep it. And the LORD God commanded the man, saying, of every tree of the garden thou mayest freely eat: but of the tree of The Knowledge of Good and Evil, thou shalt not eat of it: for in the Day that thou eatest thereof thou shalt surely die." Genesis 2: 15-17.

The law of the Garden of Eden was simple but had consequence for disobedience. The commandment from God from the creation of time, was to keep the garden, or to take care of what God had given mankind, God always wants us to take care of all that he has given to us, but the second part of the command was the command of what must not be done. God had given mankind clear instruction on what they were to do as well as what they were not to do. He said, "Do not take of the tree of The Knowledge of Good and Evil," that was met with a consequence, "thou shalt surely die." Disobedience to God's law is sin. Sin caused a curse on the whole world and its inhabitants. The curse to the ground was that it would bring forth thorns and thistles. The animals were cursed with fear of mankind. Sin's curse caused hate and sorrow. Sin's curse caused work and sweat. Sin also caused the curse of death. These of sin's curses if had been alone, and no more, it would have made the world to be a place most horrid, but the greatest of sin's curse was a separation from God. For mankind to be separated from God was a fate worse than death, without the plan of redemption the curse was more dreadful then all the other curses, for lack of deep fellowship with God will leave you empty on the inside, leaving a wound that can only be healed by redemption. The greatest of sin's curse was the spiritual death of mankind, which led to a spiritual separation from God. Genesis 3:14-19 tells of sin's curse.

"And the LORD God said unto the serpent, because thou hast done this, thou art cursed above all cattle, and above every beast of the field; upon thy belly shalt thou go, and dust shat thou eat all the days of thy life: and I will put enmity between thee and the woman, and between thy seed and her seed; it shall bruise thy head, and thou shalt bruise his heel. Unto the woman He said, I will greatly multiply thy sorrow and thy conception; in sorrow thou shalt bring forth children; and thy desire shall be to thy husband, and he shall rule over thee. And unto Adam He said, because thou hast hearkened unto the voice of thy wife, and hast eaten of the tree, of which I commanded thee, saying, thou shalt not eat of it: cursed is the ground for thy sake; in sorrow shalt thou eat of it all the days of thy life; thorns also and thistles shall it bring forth to thee; and thou shalt eat the herb of the field; in the sweat of thy face shalt thou eat bread, till thou return unto the ground; for out of it wast thou taken: for dust thou art, and unto dust shalt thou return."

Sin's cost is death. The price is paid by physical death, (unto dust shalt thou return) and spiritual death, Romans

6:23. ("For the wages of sin is death.") sin separates mankind from God and from God's paradise. Genesis chapter three tells us of the first separation.

"So, He drove out the man; and placed at the east of the garden of Eden Cherubims, and a flaming sword which turned every way, to keep the way of the Tree of Life." Genesis 3:24.

The sin of mankind separates man from his peaceful existence. Disobedience to God always takes our peace and separates us from the face of God and from the voice of God.

Psalm 66:18 says, "If I regard iniquity in my heart, the Lord will not hear me:"

Isaiah 59:2 says, "But your iniquities have separated between you and your God, and your sins have hid His face from you, that He will not hear."

Frist John 1:5 says, "God is light, and in Him is no darkness at all."

The Holiness of God cannot stand in the presence of sin. As much as darkness cannot dwell with light, so God's Holiness cannot dwell where there is sin. Holy is a characteristic of God that saturates all His other attributes. He is Holy in his power. He is Holy in His love. He is holy in His judgement. He is Holy in His faithfulness. **God is Holy!**

Isaiah also declares, "And one cried unto another, and said, Holy, Holy, Holy, is the LORD of hosts: the whole earth is full of His glory." Isaiah 6:3.

We have seen that sin, from the very beginning of time, has separated mankind from God, because God is Holy, but God is a loving God and wants mankind to dwell with Him. He wants to have a relationship with each individual soul. Jesus tells of God's love for all of mankind when He said to Nicodemus, "For God so loved the world, that He gave His only begotten Son, that whosoever believeth in Him should not perish, but have everlasting life. For God sent not His Son into the world to condemn the world; but that the world through Him might be saved." John 3:16-17.

The reason for the resurrection is the redemption of the world. We see that all creation is brought under sin's curse. It tells us in Romans, "For we know that the whole creation groaneth and travaileth in pain together until now." Romans 8:22. Someday all of creation will be brought back to perfection, as it was at the time of the garden. In Revelation 21:1-4 it tells us, "And I saw a new heaven and a new earth: for the first heaven and the first earth were passed away; and there was no more sea. And I, John saw the holy city, new Jerusalem, coming down from God out of heaven prepared as a bride adorned for her husband. And I heard a great voice out of heaven saying, "Behold, the tabernacle of God is with men, and he will dwell with them, and they shall be His people, and God himself shall be with them, and be their God. And God shall wipe away all tears from their eyes; and there shall be no more death, neither sorrow, nor crying, neither shall they be any more pain: for the former things are passed away."

Let us look at Isaiah 11:6 to see another of sin's curses that one day will be lifted. "The wolf also shall dwell with the lamb, and the leopard shall lie down with the kid; and the calf and the young lion and the fatling together; and a little child shall lead them." God will restore all things that was lost in paradise because of sin's curse. The fear of the animals will be lifted. The world will be at peace with God who created it, but best of all the unobstructed presence of the Great I Am will dwell with mankind, and all hurting, and tears and sorrow will be no more. This will be all because of the power of redemption, by the power of the resurrection.

We can have some of the power of the resurrection infused into our lives today, because of God's love. Frist John 4:9-10 tells us, "In this was manifested the love of God toward us, because that God sent his only begotten Son into the world, that we might live through him. Herein is love, not that we loved God, but that he loved us, and sent his Son to be the propitiation for our sins."

God sent His Son to be an atoning sacrifice for our sin. We are hopeless and cannot help ourselves to come near unto God. Therefore, God sent His Son to be the perfect sacrifice so that we may receive the free gift of salvation.

Romans 5:8 also gives insight into God's amazing love it reads, "But God commendeth his love toward us, in that, while we were yet sinners, Christ died for us." God loved us when we were sinners, He died in our place because we needed to die for our sin. He took the punishment for our sin. When I think about Jesus taking our punishment on the cross, I am reminded of a happening from my childhood. The story as told by my sister, that there was a time when she was going to be in trouble for something that was done, and at our house, punishment from the hand of dad was severe. I not wanting her to be punished took the blame, and the punishment that she would have received. As the years passed my memory had changed the same story, but it was her taking the punishment for me. So, it shows the love we had for each other. What God has done is so much greater, he took our punishment of death that we might have life. Christ so loved you and me that He died in our place.

1 John 3:1 tells us of God's love, "Behold, what manner of love the Father hath bestowed upon us, that we should be called the sons of God:" The cross shows God's love bridges the gap between sinful man and the Holiness of God. It brings us into the family of God.

Death is the penalty for sin. So, we see that as it says in Hebrews 9:22, "without shedding of blood is no remission.", but that blood must be human blood. God's law required it. Genesis states that, "and surely your blood of your lives will I require" Genesis 9:5. It must also be holy blood. The sacrifice of all the lambs that were in the time of the Old

Testament sacrifices were not sufficient to be the atonement for our sin, but John The Baptist looked at Jesus and saw the sinless Lamb of God and said, "Behold the Lamb of God which taketh away the sin of the world." John 1:29.

It reads in Hebrews 9:11-14 that Jesus has become our sacrifice. "But Christ being come an high priest of good things to come, by a greater and more perfect tabernacle, not made with hands, that is to say, not of this building; Neither by the blood of goats and calves, but by his own blood he entered in once into the holy place, having obtained eternal redemption for us. For if the blood of bulls and of goats, and the ashes of an heifer sprinkling the unclean, sanctifieth to the purifying of the flesh: How much more shall the blood of Christ, who through the eternal Spirit offered himself without spot to God, purge your conscience from dead works to serve the living God?

Christ was born of the virgin Mary and the original sin of mankind was not passed down upon Him. The fall of original sin was passed through the seed of man. Romans 5:12 tells us, "Wherefore, as by one man sin entered into the world, and death by sin; and so, death passed upon all men, for all have sinned."

Jesus was sinless from His birth, Matthew 1:20 says, "But while he thought on these things, behold, the angel of the Lord appeared unto him in a dream, saying, Joseph, thou son of David, fear not to take unto you Mary thy wife: for that which is conceived in her is of the Holy Ghost." Therefore, He is the sinless sacrifice of God's spotless lamb to take away the sin of the world.

But wait why wasn't the death of Christ sufficient to bridge the gap from our sinfulness to God's Holiness? Why the need for the resurrection? Life must come from life. The risen Christ took the power from death. The curse of sin is death. He became mankind's substitute for sin's punishment, but He also became the victor over death for all mankind. Christ needed not only to die for our sin, but He also needed to arise victorious over death, that we can have eternal life. William R. Newell penned the words that says it so well, "O the love that drew salvation's plan! O the grace that brought it down to man! O the mighty gulf that God did span at Calvary!" (Newell, At Calvary 1895)

Chapter two:
The Power to change

One of the greatest powers of the resurrection is power to live a changed life. The new life of a Christian is a changed life. In 2 Corinthians 5:17 it says, "Therefore if any man be in Christ, he is a new creature: old things are passed away; behold, all things are become new." God does a work in the heart of mankind at the time of salvation that makes that person not to walk in darkness, but in the bright shining light of God's forgiveness. The power of the resurrection is the power to live a changed life, we no longer live in the life of sin from which Christ has freed us. John 8:36, tells us, "If the Son therefore shall make you free, ye shall be free indeed." we have the power to be free from sin.

In his song Glorious Freedom Haldor Lillenas beautifully pinned it, "Glorious freedom! Wonderful freedom! No more in the chains of sin I repine! Jesus the glorious Emancipator now and forever He shall be mine." (Glorious Freedom, Lillenas 1917) Praise God we can have glorious freedom! When we were sinners, we were chained to sin. We could not free ourselves from sin's power. We would keep coming back to the same sin again and again, because we were once enslaved to sin. The power of the resurrected Christ can break the chains of sin and set us free.

The power of the resurrection gives the Christians the power to live without sinning. This power comes from the power of Christ living in us and us being crucified. Galatians says, "I am crucified with Christ: nevertheless, I live; yet not I, but Christ liveth in me: and the life that I now live I live in the flesh I live by faith of the Son of God, who loved me and gave Himself for me." Galatians 2:20. Christ now lives in me! I now am dead to my old life of sin. Dead to hate. Dead to pride. Dead to self. Dead to the ways of the world. I am now alive to love! Love deeply and purely, the love of Christ flowing through me.

What makes this change possible? A changed heart. Psalm 51:10 says, "Create in me a clean heart, O God; and renew a right spirit within me." the power to change from sinfulness to an obedient life in Christ, because we are dead to sin as the apostle Paul wrote to the Romans. It says, "Likewise reckon ye also yourselves to be dead indeed unto sin, but alive unto God through Jesus Christ our Lord. Let not sin therefore reign in your mortal body, that ye should obey it in the lusts thereof." Romans 6:11-12. If you are dead physically you will no longer have an appetite for your favorite food, or pastime. Your appetites are dead. So, spiritually when you have been crucified with Christ old appetites have been put to death, and new appetites have taken their place, now you hunger for the things of God. You are changed. You are dead to sin but alive unto God, not letting sin be your slave master. Paul also says in the same chapter, "For he that is dead is freed from sin." Romans 6:7. He also says in chapter six verses one and two, "What shall we say then? Shall we continue in sin, that grace may abound? God forbid. How shall we that are dead to sin, live any longer therein?" Peter likewise wrote, in 1Peter 2:24 it reads, "Who His own self bares our sins in His body on the tree, that we, being dead to sins, should live unto righteousness:" Peter says dead to sin, but alive to morality. Peter and Paul taught that Christians live changed lives. The apostle John also tells us about not sinning when he writes in 1John 2:1 "My little children, these things write unto you that ye sin not." The power of the resurrection is the power to live without sinning day by day. For John continues to tell us in 1John 3:8-9 it boldly states, "He that committeth sin is of the devil; for the devil sinneth from the beginning. For this purpose the Son of God was manifested, that He might destroy the works of the devil. Whosoever is born of God doth not commit sin; for His seed remaineth in him: and he cannot sin, because he is born of God." John writes clearly that when you have been born into the family of God, you are no longer a child of the devil, and no longer sinning, because of the power of the resurrection.

Christ will help us to live changed lives. It says in Galatians 5:24-25 "And they that are Christ's have crucified the flesh with the affections and lusts. If we live in the Spirit, let us also walk in the Spirit." You see Christ helps us to walk in the Spirit and that changes us. It is a daily walk of renewal. Paul writes in 2Corinthians 4:16 "For which cause we faint not; but though our outward man perish, yet the inward man is renewed day by day." Our inward man is renewed by of devotional life and prayer. God keeps us renewed also by leading us as it says in psalms, "Psalm 139:23-24 Search me, O God, and know my heart: try me, and know my thoughts: And see if there be any wicked way in me and lead me in the way everlasting. Dorothy A. Thrupp, in 1836 penned the words "Savior like a shepherd lead us much we need thy tender care." And that is what God does for us, he leads day by day. We are changed to become more like our heavenly Father. We see a boy born into a family, helpless at first but he is growing. Soon he will walk on his own, but you will see him have some family traits, he may stand just like his father, or he may have light hair like his mother, it is because he is part of the family. He will become a man someday for he is changing. All his changes did not happen all at once, but little by little. He became alive, however, instantaneously. We know that he did not run even after his first birthday, but soon he will run and be everywhere seemingly all at the same time. The life of the Christian is instantaneous at the new birth, but the transformation is also a step at a time, day by day.

It tells us in the book of 2Corinthians 3:18 "But we all, with open face beholding as in a glass the glory of the Lord, are changed into the same image from glory to glory, even as by the Spirit of the Lord." We should expect the world to look on us and see Christ in us. In our behavior, our actions and reactions, we should look like Christ. We have been changed, by the power of the resurrection.

Paul wrote to the church at Ephesus, telling them that they had put on the new man. It reads, "That ye put off concerning the former conversation the old man, which is corrupt according to the deceitful lusts; and be renewed in the spirit of your mind; and that ye put on the new man, which after God is created in righteousness and true holiness." Ephesians 4:22-24. The new man is new on the inside. We are new in our talk; we no longer say the dirty words or suggestive talk. We use our speech to the glory of God. We do not gossip or speak to harm others. Now the new man will pray for others. We will not lie but be truthful and honest. The new man will not be involved in practices of sin. We are new in our actions and reactions. All our actions are to the glory of God.

He tells us that the old man is put off and the new man is put on, the new man is created by God, but must be renewed.

We will run dry if not renewed, by daily drawing near to God by daily finding time to fellowship with Him.

The power of the resurrection is the power to be an overcomer. 1John 4:4 says, "Ye are of God, little children, and have overcome them: because greater is He that is in you, than he that is in the world." God has given us power to be overcomers. Power to be free from the chains of sin.

Let me tell you of changed lives. People who have been set free by the power of the resurrection. One was a Prostitute, a sex slave and a drug slave. Then one day Jesus came into her life, no longer bound by the chains of sin she became a shining example. She was giving her life helping others out of the life that had enslaved her.

Another was a man that was into drugs and found himself in prison for the life that he had chosen. Generations of alcoholism had haunted his family. Then Jesus passed by, and a preacher came to hold a jail service, and the Gospel message got to his soul, and he became a new creature in Christ Jesus, old things passed, and all things became new. Many of his friends from his past had said that it was just jailhouse religion and that he would turn back to the old ways. They did not know that God had made a great change in his life. God is still making changes in him. God is still changing lives by the power of the resurrection.

CHAPTER THREE:
THE POWER TO FORGIVE

Only through the power of the resurrected Christ, can we truly forgive others when we have been wronged. Jesus said when He was preaching, on the sermon on the mount, in Matthew 6:14-15, "For if ye forgive men their trespasses, your heavenly Father will also forgive you: but if ye forgive not men their trespasses, neither will your Father forgive your trespasses." Jesus said that forgiveness given to those who have wronged us is a must. It is not optional. Hurt many times goes deep. Sin can cause deep emotional pain when someone we have trusted have sinned against us. We can only forgive others through the power of prayer. If someone has hurt you deeply, give it to the one who cares the most, give it to Jesus.

The Power of the Resurrection is also the power to love your enemies. Jesus said, as well when preaching the sermon on the Mount in Matthew 5:45-47 "That ye may be the children of your Father which is in heaven: for He maketh his sun to rise on the evil and on the good, and sendeth rain on the just and on the unjust. For if ye love them which love you, what reward have ye? do not even the publicans the same? And if ye salute your brethren only, what do ye more than others? do not even the publicans so?" We are to love are enemies. I think that I can love my friend John because John is much like me. We are alike in a lot of ways. What about someone who is different than me can I love them? What if we don't agree on doctrine, or on politics? Can I still love them? Jesus hated sin, but He loved the sinner. He knew that each sinner could change by the power of the resurrection. What about loving people who have been taught to hate me, because of my race or anything else in which they hate me. There are people who hate you for no reason. You can love them, by the Power of the Resurrection. Jesus also preached that Christians were to literally turn the other cheek, in Matthew it reads, "Matthew 5:38-39 Ye have heard that it hath been said, an eye for an eye, and a tooth for a tooth: But I say unto you, that ye resist not evil: but whosoever shall smite thee on thy right cheek, turn to him the other also." Is this Scripture to be taken literally? I think that it is what Jesus taught. It is the Power to forgive. It is the Power of the Resurrection. Some people might say that we don't know what has happened to them. It is too hard to forgive. It would be, but for the Power of the Resurrection. Someone might say that they are willing to forgive, unless you harm their family, their children. Does God have the power to let you forgive when your children have been harmed by actions or by words of others? Can God have the power to help you forgive when you have been hurt by people in your family or in the Church? **Yes, the Power of the Resurrection covers hurts that are that deep!**

Paul also wrote to the church at Colossae, about forgiveness. In Colossians 3:12-13 he writes, "Put on therefore, as the elect of God, holy and beloved, bowels of mercies, kindness, humbleness of mind, meekness, longsuffering; forbearing one another, and forgiving one another, if any have a quarrel against any: even as Christ forgave you, so also do ye." Unforgiveness will eat like a cancer. Paul started in this passage of his letter to the Colossians talking about, having mercy. It is a progressive passage each step leading to the next. Mercy is connected to kindness which leads us to humbleness. When we begin to show mercy, it makes us think less about ourselves and more about others. That opens the door to forgiveness because forgiveness flows from the heart of love. We are to forgive others with the same readiness that Christ has forgiven us. We were at onetime enemies of Christ it says in Romans 5:10, "For if, when we were enemies, we were reconciled to God by the death of his Son," being enemies Christ died for us. The sermon on the Mount teaches us to love our enemies. The songwriter has penned the words, "love that covers the faults of a brother, love that will cause us to love one another, love divine love coming down from the Father, Lord, give me more of this love." (Give Me More of This Love, Author unknown) we all need more of that love.

Jesus teaches more about forgiveness on the Sermon on the Mount, in Matthew 7:12, He teaches us to do unto others as we would have them do unto us. This we call the golden rule. He continues to teach us that the way to new life is a strait way. In Matthew 7:13-14 He says, "Enter ye in at the strait gate: for wide is the gate, and broad is the way that leads to destruction, and many there be which go in thereat: because strait is the gate, and narrow is the way, which leads unto life, and few there be that find it." The strait gate and narrow way is the way of forgiveness for others. The broad way and wide gate is the way of unforgiveness. It is a way that leads to destruction. The broad way is the way of revenge. Unforgiveness will eat at you like a cancer. Revenge is not a dish best served cold; it is a dish best not served at all. We cannot forgive others without the forgiveness of the resurrected Christ active in our lives.

We have talked about the power to forgive others when they have wronged you, but now let us look at the power to ask others to forgive us when we have done them wrong. In the gospel of Matthew 5:23-24 it reads, "Therefore, if thou bring thy gift to the altar, and there rememberest that thy brother hath ought against thee; leave there thy gift before the altar and go thy way; first be reconciled to thy brother, and then come and offer thy gift." It is hard to say, "I'm sorry, or I was wrong, please forgive me." God's plan is to make your wrongs right quickly, and not to wait until people are hurting. In Matthew 5:25 Jesus says, "Agree with thine adversary quickly, whiles thou art in the way with him; lest at any time the adversary deliver thee to the judge, and the judge deliver thee to the officer, and thou be cast into prison." Christians should always be ready to ask for others to forgive them, quickly or the wound will be infected over time and the healing of relationships will never be mended.

The gospel of Luke tells of a man named Zacchaeus, and Luke says that he wanted to see Jesus, and when he had an encounter with The Christ, he was a changed man. He was transformed by the power of God and wanted to make restitution. It says in Luke 19:8-9, "And Zacchaeus stood, and said unto the Lord; Behold, Lord, the half of my goods I give to the poor; and if I have taken anything from any man by false accusation, I restore him fourfold. And Jesus said unto him, this day is salvation come to this house, forsomuch as he also is a son of Abraham." This clearly teaches that when we have wronged others we need to ask for forgiveness and to make our wrongs right. Jesus teaches us that we can have both the power to forgive others when they have wronged us, and we can have the power to ask for forgiveness from those we have wronged. It is the power of the resurrection working in our lives.

Chapter Four:
The Power to Witness

The disciples at the cross were fearful. The one whom they had trusted to be the chosen Messiah the Savior of the world was crucified. Christ, however, had promised to give unto them power when the Holy Spirit came. In Acts 1:8 it says, "But ye shall receive power, after that the Holy Ghost is come upon you: and ye shall be witnesses unto me both in Jerusalem, and in all Judaea, and in Samaria, and unto the uttermost part of the earth." The power came from the Holy Ghost on the day of Pentecost. It was the power to witness boldly to the grace of God through the resurrected Christ. The disciples were fearful at the cross, but after the Holy Spirit came upon them, they witnessed boldly for Christ. Acts 4:31 tells us about their witnessing. "And when they had prayed, the place was shaken where they were assembled together; and they were all filled with the Holy Ghost, and they spake the word of God with boldness." They had been threatened to not preach about Jesus, but they had the boldness of the resurrected Christ. You will also find in the book of Acts chapter two about the bold preaching on the day of Pentecost. It takes more than human boldness to stand for the gospel, in the face of death. Acts chapters six and seven tell us of a man full of the Holy Ghost, who preached Christ until the mob stoned him to death. He would not be stopped.

Paul when writing to the Ephesians, asked that they would pray for him, that he would speak boldly. "And for me, that utterance may be given unto me, that I may open my mouth boldly, to make known the mystery of the gospel, for I am an ambassador in bonds: that therein I may speak boldly, as I ought to speak." Ephesians 6:19-20. If Paul needed the Church to pray for him to have boldness, then we also need to have prayer too for boldness.

The Bible gives instructions about witnessing. It tells in the book of First Peter, that we should be ready to tell others of the hope that we have in the resurrected Christ. It says, "But sanctify the Lord God in your hearts: and be ready always to give an answer, to every man that asketh you a reason of the hope that is in you with meekness and fear:" 1 Peter 3:15. We are to be ready to tell others boldly, but with meekness, not with arrogance for it is not your own power that we have this hope.

Peter tells us to be ready to answer, but anyone knows the best answers come from study. In 2Timothy 2:15 it reads,

"Study to show thyself approved unto God, a workman that needeth not to be ashamed, rightly dividing the word of truth." We are to be a working witness. We are employed in the work of telling the gospel story to the world. Therefore, we should know what is in the word of God so that we might be bold to tell of the power of the risen Christ.

Have you ever felt guilty about your witnessing, or not witnessing because you don't think that you measure up to the witnessing of others? You may not witness the same as others. Bible scholars have seen in the New Testament six distinct types or styles of evangelism. Each type or style fits different personalities.

One, the direct confrontational approach. In this style you will be boldly confronting strangers about their soul condition. We see Peter as this type, his direct approach on the day of Pentecost in Acts 2:36 it reads, "Therefore let all the house of Israel know assuredly, that God hath made that same Jesus, whom ye crucified, both Lord and Christ." This approach is both direct and confrontational, which is perfectly in step with the way God had made Peter.

The next style of evangelism we will look at is the intellectual approach. With this style the Christian will focus on laying out well-reasoned arguments for the evidence for Christianity. Paul used this style of evangelism. It reads in Acts 17:2-3, "And Paul, as his manner was, went in unto them, and three sabbath days reasoned with them out of the scriptures, opening and alleging, that Christ must needs have suffered, and risen again from the dead; and that this Jesus, whom I preach unto you, is Christ." We see this style of evangelism fits Paul because he was a scholar.

The third type or style of evangelism that we will look at is the relational approach. We see in the book of Luke 5:29, that Levi (Matthew) had made a great feast and invited those who he was acquainted with to have a meal with him. You can see that he had used his table for a place to bring people to Jesus. Many of those people were perhaps his coworkers and their families.

The style of evangelism that we will look at now is the invitational approach. The invitational approach was used by the Samaritan woman after her conversion her testimony was to the whole town. In the gospel of John 4:28-29 it reads, "The woman then left her waterpot, and went her way into the city, and saith to the men, come, see a man, which told me all things that ever I did: is not this the Christ?

God uses the style of testimony evangelism to reach the hearts of others. In the gospel of Luke, it tells of a life changed by the power of Christ. A man had been tormented with devils, who had been bound by chains and dwelled in the tombs. Luke tells us that Jesus told him to stay at home and tell others about what God had done for him. Luke 8:38-40 tells it, "Now the man out of whom the devils were departed besought Him that he might be with him: but Jesus sent him away, saying, return to thine own house, and show how great things God hath done unto thee. And he went his way and published throughout the whole city how great things Jesus had done unto him. And it came to pass, that when Jesus was returned, the people gladly received Him: for they were all waiting for Him." This is a great example of God using the power of testimony evangelism to change the hearts of others. For it reads in verse 37 that the whole multitude asked Jesus to depart out of their country, but after they saw the change and heard his testimony then all the people gladly welcomed Jesus back when He returned.

The style that uses the serving approach in evangelism is seen in the life of Dorcas it reads about how she used her servant's heart to bring others to Christ, in Acts 9:36-39. Showing Christ's love to others by doing good deeds of kindness is a lovely way to evangelize.

Whatever the style of evangelism that God gives you to use we are instructed by Jesus to let our light shine, so that we may glorify God. Jesus tells us in Matthew 5:16 "Let your light so shine before men, that they may see your good works, and glorify your Father which is in Heaven." This reminds me of an illustration that God had given me. I was in a Christmas Eve candlelight service. When we came into the service, we were each given an unlit candle. We then made our way to our seats. The room was dark. The service then begun and at last the time had come to light our candles. The pastor had lit his candle off a large candle, it was the only lit candle in the room. After he had fire on his candle, he then lit the candle of the one nearest to him in the Church. The person who had just received the fire on their candle in turn shared their fire with the next in the room. This went on each sharing their fire with the one who was nearest, until at last all the candles were lit.

The first candle that had to start the fire burning in all the other candles symbolized Jesus, the light of the world. The other candles shared their fire with the one who were closest. We will share our fire with our closest and dearest loved ones. As each follower of Christ, shears their light they give someone else a light that can be shared. When we let our light shine, we give glory to the Father who has given us new life.

The Great Commission that Jesus gave to the Church in Matthew 28:18-20 gives us the responsibility to witness to the power of the resurrection. It says, "And Jesus came and spake unto them, saying, all power is given unto me in Heaven and in Earth. Go ye therefore, and teach all nations, baptizing them in the name of the Father, and of the Son, and of the Holy Ghost: teaching them to observe all things whatsoever I have commanded you and, lo, I am with you always, even unto the end of the world. Amen.

We are to be witnesses by teaching, the commands of God. We need to teach of the risen Christ and tell what His power has done in our lives. The passage tells us that Jesus will help us to be witnesses, giving us His power, because He is with us, and His power will go with us always. The need to witness is well said in the words of a song by A.C. Palmer, "Ready to go, ready to bear, ready to watch and pray, ready to stand aside and give till He shall clear the way." (Ready, Palmer, 1845) We need to wait until Christ leads when we witness, but we need to be ready to answer the call to witness to the power of the resurrection.

We need to be ready to witness, whenever, and wherever God leads us. We also should be wise enough to let God use our own unique style to tell the gospel story. Let us trust God to give us the power to witness, to the power of the resurrection, working through us, in the way that best fits who God made us.

Chapter Five:
The Power of The Comforter

The power of the resurrection is found in the power of the Comforter. Jesus said that it was necessary that he go away that the Comforter would come. Jesus tells us in John, 16:7, "Nevertheless I tell you the truth; it is expedient for you that I go away, for if I go not away, the Comforter will not come unto you; but if I depart, I will send Him unto you."

William Greathouse has beautiful insights on the person of the Holy Spirit in his book *The Fullness of the Spirit,* it reads, "The Resurrection is the assurance of the divine victory over sin, death, and hell, and the pledge to us of a living Christ. The Holy Spirit came to impart God. The Holy Spirit came to apply to our hearts the benefits of Christ's redemptive sufferings. He exists to act within. His it is to enter into the recesses of the human spirit and to work from within the subjectivity of man. From within our human being the Spirit vitalizes, stabilizes, renews, admonishes, warns, recalls, interprets, enlightens, guides, and gives us comfort (or strength). He is God in His special activity and agency of secret invasion and invisible occupation. He is the sanctifying Spirit-making us holy even as the Father is holy.

If God's self-revelation climaxed in Jesus' life, death, and resurrection, His self-impartation climaxed in His coming through the Spirit at Pentecost to indwell and sanctify His people. Jesus is God *with* us; the Holy Spirit is God *in* us.

One name given by Jesus to the Holy Spirit is Comforter. The Greek word Paraclete so translated means "one called to stand beside us." The exact English equivalent is the word Advocate. The Holy Spirit, Jesus promised, shall be with us-in us-to counsel us, to guide us, to help us, to console us in the dark night of suffering and sorrow." (William M. Greathouse, Fullness of The Spirit, p 63,64)

The power of the Comforter is sent unto us by the heavenly Father. We need the Comforter; the heavenly Father knows that we need the power of one that comes by our side to help. Life comes at us like a storm, when the storm of life's troubles come, like sickness, loss of financial stability, death of a loved one, or any heartache that may come, the Comforter is standing by our side through the storm.

In John 14:16 Jesus says, "And I will pray the Father, and He shall give you another Comforter, that He may abide with you forever;" The Comforter comes to abide with us. He will abide to be our helper, and our guide. When Herbert Buffum wrote the words to the song, *He Abides* he must have had a personal relationship with the one who comes by our side, to be our helper, when he writes, "He abides, He abides, Hallelujah, He abides with me! I'm rejoicing night and day as I walk the narrow way, for the Comforter abides with me." (Buffum, 1879) we too can sing Hallelujah! He abides!

Romans 8:11 tells us the marvelousness about the Comforter, it reads, "But if the Spirit of Him that raised up Jesus from the dead dwell in you, he that raised up Christ from the dead shall also quicken your mortal bodies by His Spirit that dwelleth in you." The word quicken means to make alive. We will be made alive in the first resurrection when Christ raptures His bride, but the power of the Comforter will quicken us into new life, immediately when He comes into our lives. We are living in the new life now! The power of the Comforter will make us spiritually alive by the power of the resurrection!

In John 16:13 Jesus tells us that the Comforter comes to guide us. It says, "Howbeit when He, the Spirit of truth, is come, He will guide you into all truth: for He shall not speak of Himself; but whatsoever He shall hear, that shall He speak; and He will show you things to come." This passage reveals unto us two things.

One, that the Holy Spirit comes to guide. He will guide us into all truth if we listen to Him. People have gone astray after false doctrine because they have never received the gift of the Comforter, the gift of guidance. When we feel pulled by dynamic preaching into themes not supported by scripture, we are not listening to the voice of the Holy Spirit. The Holy Spirit will always lead us into teachings which are fully aligned with God's holy word. Teaching or preaching which is not in line with holy scripture is false doctrine.

The next thing that is revealed to us in this passage is how the Holy Spirit will show us things to come. Light given to us by the Holy Spirit is not given all at once but step by step the spirit will guide us. Day by day the Comforter will show us God's will for our lives.

The Comforter not only comes into our lives to come alongside us to help us, but also to make us more alive than we have ever been because He lives in us. The Holy Spirit will give you power when He comes into your life. As it says in Acts 1:8 "But ye shall receive power, after that the Holy Ghost is come upon you;" Jesus did not leave us powerless, because He has given the power of the one who braves every storm, right by our side.

Chapter six:
The Keeping Power of the Resurrection

The Bible tells us that we can be overcomers. We can overcome because of the keeping power of the resurrection. It tells us in 1John 4:4 "Ye are of God, little children, and have overcome them; because greater is He that is in you, than he that is in the world." In us is the keeping power of the Resurrection because we have the one who arose from the dead, and is alive forevermore, the living Christ!

The Bible goes on to tell us we can do all things through the power of Christ. In Philippians 4:13 it reads, "I can do all things through Christ which strengtheneth me." It is Christ who gives us strength, His strength. We need not to be weak it is strength from the Almighty. The God of all the universe, the God who is always in control, it is Him that has given us strength.

The Bible tells us that we are to be overcomers, but what is it that we are to overcome? In Romans 12:21 Paul says,

"Be not overcome of evil, but overcome evil with good." So, it is evil that we are overcoming. The evil comes from the evil one the devil. Ephesians 4:27 explains, "Neither give place to the devil." The devil wants to derail us from our Christian walk, but we can resist the devil. It tells us in James 4:7-10 the way to overcome, "Submit yourselves therefore to God, resist the devil, and he will flee from you. Draw nigh to God, and He will draw nigh to you. Cleanse your hands ye sinners; and purify your heart, ye double minded. Be afflicted, and mourn, and weep: let your laughter be turned to mourning, and your joy to heaviness. Humble yourselves in the sight of the Lord, and He shall lift you up." The way to be an overcomer is to submit to God. Be willing to let Him lead.

The next step is to resist the devil. Christians need to stay away from places where the devil controls the battlefield. Resist evil thoughts that the devil will put in your mind, by purposely keeping your mind on heavenly things, such as, Bible verses, Christian hymns, prayer needs, and God's goodness.

This will naturally bring you to the next step in resisting the devil, by drawing near to God. To draw near to God, we must open our heart to Him, as David did in Psalm 139:23-24, "Search me, O God, and know my heart: try me and know my thoughts: and see if there be any wicked way in me and lead me in the way everlasting." We need God to bring the search light to make sure that we have nothing that would crowd God out of being first place in our lives. Draw near to God by humbling yourself in prayer. This will help you to stand in the time of temptation.

The power to stand and be an overcomer in the face of temptation comes from the power of the Resurrection. In Galatians 5:1 it says, "Stand fast therefore in the liberty wherewith Christ has made us free and be not entangled again with the yoke of bondage." The word, therefore, refers back to chapter four where it tells us that Christ was come that we might become the children of the promise, we have the freedom that comes from being born into the family of God. We have the privileges of being born into the family of God which gives us the strength to stand with God's keeping grace. Stand and don't give up! I like the way P. P. Bliss put it when he penned the words in the song, he wrote, *Dare to Be a Daniel,* "Standing by a purpose true, heeding God's command, honor them, the faithful few! All hail to Daniel's band! Dare to be a Daniel! Dare to stand alone! Dare to have a purpose firm! Dare to make it known!" (Bliss, 1873) God gives Christians keeping power. The power to be an overcomer. The power of the resurrected Christ.

Chapter Seven:
The Power of Intercession

In this chapter I want to look at power of intercessory prayer. One of the greatest powers of the Resurrection is the power of intercessory prayer. It can be said that there are five different types of prayer.

1. Worship – this is praying to exalt the greatness of God
2. Petition – this is praying to ask God for things that we need, it can be both spiritual and physical needs.
3. Thanksgiving – this type of praying is thanking God for blessings received.
4. Praise – this praying acknowledges God for who He is and simply because He exist.
5. Intercession – this is the type of praying for the needs of others.

The power of intercession cannot be if it is not for the power of the resurrection, because Christ lives, and is interceding for us we can be like Christ and intercede for others.

Let us look at what the Bible says about intercessory prayer. The Lord Jesus said in what is called His High Priestly prayer, in John 17:9, "I pray for them: I pray not for the world, but for them which thou hast given me; for they are thine." There before the cross, Christ prays for the Church. What does Christ pray about?

He prays that the Church will have unity. John 17:11 "that they may be one, as we are." God's plan is that the Church be unified not divided. The Church can be one, by the power of the Resurrection.

Christ prays that the Church might have joy. In John 17:13, "And now come I to thee; and these things I speak in the world, that they might have joy fulfilled in themselves." The Christian way is a way of joy. It is not a sad mule-faced religion, but a happy joyous way.

Christ prays that the Church will be kept from evil. In John 17:15, "I pray not that thou shouldest take them out of the world, but that thou shouldest keep them from the evil." Here we see that Christians can be kept in this evil and wicked world. We are not taken away from the world, we are kept so that its evil doesn't affect us.

He prays that the Church will be sanctified, in John 17:19 it reads, "And for their sakes I sanctify myself, that they also might be sanctified through the truth." Christ wants the Church to be sanctified. He wants Christians to be set apart for holy use. He wants Christians to be holy, to be pure and God-like in heart. He prays that Christians will have perfect love.

Christ prays that the Church will be able to behold His glory and be with Him where he dwells. It reads in John 17:24, "Father I will that they also, whom thou hast given me, be with me where I am that they may behold my glory, which thou hast given me: for thou lovedst me before the foundation of the world." Christ longs that we the Church, His bride, will be with Him and behold His glory.

Christ is praying that the Church will be one in unity, that it will be perfect, that it will be with Him in Heaven. This is what Christ prayed for the Church just before the cross.

Christ's intercession did not end there, it reads in Romans 8:34, "Who is he that condemneth? It is Christ that died, yea rather, that is risen again, who is even at the right hand of God, who maketh intercession for us." It also tells us in the book of Hebrews how Jesus is now making intercession for us. It reads in Hebrews 7:25, "Wherefore He is able to save them to the uttermost that come unto God by Him, seeing He ever liveth to maketh intercession for them."

Christ is praying for us as our High Priest. Hebrews 4:14-16 reads, "Seeing then that we have a great High Priest that is passed into the heavens, Jesus the Son of God, let us hold fast our profession. For we have not an High Priest which cannot be touched with the feeling of our infirmities; but was in all points tempted like as we are, yet without sin. Let us therefore come boldly unto the throne of grace, that we may obtain mercy, and find grace to help in time of need." The resurrected Christ is actively praying for us. What is He praying about? One thing that Jesus is praying about is that we hold fast to our faith. Next that we will be overcomers in time of temptation.

Lastly that we will have grace to help. Grace to lift us up in time of spiritual need. In the book of First Peter 5:7 it reads, "Casting all your care upon Him; for he careth for you." The Church has the assurance of the power of the resurrected Christ interceding for us. I am drawn back to that old hymn of the Church written by William W. Walford, *Sweet Hour of Prayer,* "Sweet hour of prayer, sweet hour of prayer, that calls me from a world of care and bids me at my Father's throne make all my wants and wishes known! In seasons of distress and grief my soul has often found relief, and often escaped the tempter's snare by thy return, sweet hour of prayer." (Walford 1845) Christ cares about whatever concerns us. The power of the resurrection is the power of answered prayers.

The scripture also tells us to be intercessors for one another in our Christian walk. One of the greatest examples of intercessory prayer is in the book of Exodus. Moses was looking at the judgement of God upon a sinful nation. He prays for the Israelites, in the Book of Exodus 32:30-32, "And it came to pass on the morrow, that Moses said unto the people, ye have sinned a great sin: and now I will go up unto the Lord; peradventure I shall make an atonement for your sin. And Moses returned unto the Lord, and said, Oh, this people have sinned a great sin, and have made them gods of gold. Yet now, if thou wilt forgive their sin-----; and if not, blot me, I pray thee, out of thy book which thou hast written." Moses put himself between the judgement of God and a sinful nation. Moses' example of praying for a sinful nation is the pattern that we as Christians should follow today, instead of criticism let us pray. In 1Timothy it states that it is God's will that we should pray for all men. 1Timothy 2:1 it says, "I exhort therefore, that, first of all, supplications, prayers, intercessions, and giving of thanks, be made for all men;" Let us look at other scriptures to see their insight on intercessory prayer.

1Samuel 12:23, "Moreover as for me, God forbid that I should sin against the Lord in ceasing to pray for you: but I will teach you the good and the right way:"

James 5:16, "Confess your faults one to another, and pray one for another, that ye may be healed. The effectual fervent prayer of a righteous man availeth much."

Galatians 6:2, "Bear ye one another's burdens, and so fulfil the law of Christ."

As Christians it is our privilege to help our brothers and sisters, in the faith, to help carry their burdens to the one who intercedes for us all, the Lord Jesus Christ.

Chapter Eight:
The Power of the Resurrection

In the upper room set the twelve disciples, they were sitting with Jesus and had just eaten the Passover feast. The Passover meal being ended, the Lord took the place of a servant and began to wash the disciples' feet. This act by the Lord Jesus Christ was an act of love. It was to give them proof that He loved them enough to be their servant. In John 13:1 it tells of His love, it reads, "Now before the feast of the Passover, when Jesus knew that His hour was come that he should depart out of this world unto the Father, having loved his own which were in the world, He loved them unto the end." The scene was a serious scene. Jesus told them that one of them would betray Him. Their hearts were saddened. Who would betray such a friend?

The chief priests and scribes hated Jesus and they wanted Him dead. They laid a scheme how they might take Jesus when He was away from the multitude and arrest Him. Luke tells it in Luke 22:2, "And the chief priests and scribes sought hoe they might kill Him; for they feared the people." Their evil scheme was aided by Satan, Luke 22:3-6 tells the account, "Then entered Satan into Judas surnamed Iscariot, being one of the number of the twelve. And he went his way, and communed with the chief priests and captains, how he might betray Him unto them. And they were glad, and covenanted to give him money. And he promised, and sought opportunity to betray Him unto them in the absence of the multitude."

Then after they had sung a hymn, this band of followers went to the mount of Olives into the garden of Gethsemane to pray.

Jesus also went on to say that all of them would be offended because of Him. Mark 14:27 gives account and says, "And Jesus saith unto them, all ye shall be offended because of me this night: for it is written, I will smite the shepherd, and the sheep shall be scattered." Peter declared even though everyone will deny you Jesus I will stand by you! We look at Peter's bold statement and we see only Peter's denial, but the scripture also says that all the disciples said that they too would not deny the Lord. It reads in Mark 14:31, "But he (*Peter*) spake the more vehemently, if I should die with thee, I will not deny thee in any wise. Likewise also said they all." Peter as Jesus foretold did deny the Lord three times. Jesus also said that all the disciples would be offended because of Him, and it reads in Mark 14:50 after Jesus' arrest, "And they all forsook Him and fled."

Jesus and His disciples had shared the Passover, they had partaken in the first Lord's supper, that we call the last supper, Jesus had washed their feet, He had taken them into the garden to pray, Jesus had been betrayed, denied, and forsaken by those who He called His friends.

Now Jesus had been arrested by the chief priests, captains of the temple, and the elders. The religious leaders had come together to put to death the Christ, the Messiah. It was appropriate that the religious leaders would be the ones that would bring the Lamb of God to be slain. The High Priest was the only one to take the lamb to be offered on the Day of Atonement. The book of Saint John 1:29 records the testimony of John the Baptist, he writes, "The next day John seeth Jesus coming unto him, and saith, behold the Lamb of God, which taketh away the sin of the world."

The agony that Jesus went through when he was praying in the garden, the sadness that He felt being betrayed and forsaken by friends, and the pain which He endured with the beatings by the Roman soldiers as well as the pain and torment of the crucifixion, was all part of the divine will of God.

Not only was the suffering of the Lamb of God part of God's plan, but also the resurrection of the Lamb of God was necessary to bring eternal life. The lives of all who experienced the resurrection of Jesus, the Lamb of God, were forever changed.

THE POWER OF THE RESURRECTION

On that bright early resurrection morning, Mary Magdalene, Mary the mother of James, and Salome came to the sepulcher where the body of Jesus was laid, so that they might anoint the body of Jesus with spices that they had prepared. Their worry was on their problems. Their problem was a large stone, that sealed the tomb. Mark 16:2-3 tells an insight into their situation, "And very early in the morning the first day of the week, they came unto the sepulcher at the rising of the sun. And they said among themselves, who shall roll us away the stone from the door of the sepulcher?" Life can have problems, for which we have no answers, until we meet the risen Christ. Our hope is in nothing but Christ. It is the power of the resurrection that helps in the difficult situations of life, as it did for them, we read on in Mark 16:4, "And when they looked, they saw that the stone was rolled away: for it was very great." Their problem was already gone. Christ can take away our large problems.

Matthew 28:6 record the words of the angel which resound throughout the ages, "He is not here: for He is risen, as He said. Come, see the place where the Lord lay." Jesus had died on the cross, and they had laid Him in a tomb. They with all their hearts believed Him to be the promised Messiah. Now the disciples had news that Jesus is alive. Does it seem too good to be true? It does. Was He really the Christ? Can they trust what they have heard and seen?

The disciples were fearful and doubtful they were wondering about the reports that they have heard. On the road as they walked to the village of Emmaus a man came and talked with them about the events that had taken place. He reasoned with them from out of the scriptures, of all that it said concerning Christ. The man who talked with them was Jesus, and Luke 24:25-26 tells, "Then He said unto them, O fools, and slow of heart to believe all that the prophets have spoken: ought not Christ to have suffered these things, and to enter into His glory?" They did not know that the man who had talked to them was Jesus. Then after their eyes were opened to see who He was, they said, in Luke 24:32, "And they said one to another, did not our heart burn within us, while he talked with us by the way, and while he opened to us the scriptures?" The proof that Jesus was alive was in His presence. When we have an encounter with the risen Christ, we have no doubt that He is alive!

The tomb is empty even though it had been guarded by Roman soldiers, the life of the Son of God could not be held back. Jesus arose from the dead because He is the resurrection and the life. The power of the resurrection can give us a full life. The faithful who was there at Jesus' tomb were given a new life. The life that they were given was on earth, as well as in Heaven. We have a hope of a new life now, and in the first resurrection. The song that Gloria and Bill Gaither wrote sums it up, when it says, "Because He lives, I can face tomorrow; because He lives, all fear is gone. Because I know He holds the future and life is worth the living just because He lives." (Gaither, 1971)

Chapter Nine:
The Hope of the Resurrection

What is the hope of the Resurrection? The beginning to the answer to this question is found in Paul's first letter to the Thessalonians. In 1Thessalonians 4:13-18 it says, "But I would not have you to be ignorant, brethren, concerning them which are asleep, that ye sorrow not, even as others that have no hope. For if we believe that Jesus died and rose again, even so them also which sleep in Jesus will God bring with Him. For this we say unto you by the word of the Lord, that we which are alive and remain unto the coming of the Lord shall not prevent them which are asleep. For the Lord Himself shall descend from Heaven with a shout, with the voice of the archangel, and the trump of God: and the dead in Christ shall rise first then we which are alive and remain shall be caught up together with them in the clouds, to meet the Lord in the air: and so shall we ever be with the Lord. Wherefore comfort one another with these words." This hope is that the living Christ will come, and we that who have found a resting place in Jesus, will He bring us together to be His bride. If we are alive and have the power of the resurrection working in our lives, we will be taken to be with Christ or if we have been laid to rest, we will rise from the dead as did Jesus and be with Him. It also tells in 1Corinthians 6:14, "And God hath both raised up the Lord, and will also raise up us by His own power." The apostle Paul says again in 2Corinthians 4:14, "Knowing that he which raised up the Lord Jesus shall raise up us also by Jesus and shall present us with you."

Job also had this hope, it is recorded in Job 19:25-26, "For I know that my redeemer liveth, and that He shall stand at the latter day upon the earth: and though after my skin worms destroy this body, yet in my flesh shall I see God."

God will by His miraculous power, give the dead saints that have been laid to rest a glorified body, as Jesus had at the time of His resurrection. Christians will all have a glorified body that will live forever.

This new glorified body is just the beginning for the Christian. The Bible tells us in the Book of 1John 3:2-3 that we will see Jesus. John says, "Beloved, now are we the sons of God, and it doth not yet appear what we shall be: but we know that when He shall appear, we shall be like Him, for we shall see Him as He is. And every man that hath this hope in him purifies himself, even as He is pure." In the book of Acts, we read that Jesus ascending into Heaven, and as soon as Jesus was gone the angels that were still standing there told them that were gathered not to fear, because one day they will once again see Jesus. We will see Jesus as they saw Him on the day of His ascension.

The loving Son of God, who healed the sick, opened the eyes of the blind, raised the dead, comforted the brokenhearted, and brought our life from a life of darkness to a life of God's marvelous light, will be giving us a loving embrace. Dianne Wilkinson pinned the words to the song that we have heard the Cathedral Quartet sing, *We Shall See Jesus* the song says it so well, "Once on a hillside, people were gathered for Jesus had risen and soon would ascend. Then, as He blessed them, He rose to the heavens. And gave them His promise to come back again. We shall see Jesus, just as they saw Him. There is no greater promise than this. When He returns in power and glory, we shall see Jesus, we shall see Jesus, just as He is!" (Wilkinson, 1981) We will see the loving Savior that died for our sins.

The reality of Heaven is the hope of the resurrection, the hope of the bride of Christ. We have an inheritance that cannot be inherited by our mortal bodies. First Peter 1:3-5 tells us, "Blessed be the God and Father of our Lord Jesus Christ, which according to His abundant mercy hath begotten us again unto a lively hope by the resurrection of Jesus Christ from the dead, to an inheritance incorruptible, and undefiled, that fadeth not away, reserved in Heaven for you, who are kept by the power of God through faith unto salvation ready to be revealed in the last time." This inheritance is our forever home.

Gone are all the things that have ever been our enemy. The enemy of the devil, gone. The enemy of temptation, gone. The enemy of loss, gone. The enemy of death, gone. Forever in our heavenly home we will see Jesus and we will see our loved ones who have made Heaven their home. For the first time we will see love unbridled. The whole world of Heaven is a world of love. There is no hate there, this is a world without the enemies of love. The love of God is everywhere with us now, but in Heaven we also will see brotherly love unbridled, in holy love, in all who dwell there. We will see holy love in a greater degree than we have ever experienced here on earth. The hope of the resurrection is the hope of love.

Praise God! There waits for me a glad tomorrow, a glad homecoming day. The song written by James Allen Crutchfield, *Zion's Hill,* has said it very well, "There waits for me a glad tomorrow, where gates of pearl swing open wide; and when I've passed this vale of sorrow, I'll dwell upon the other side." (Crutchfield, 1923)

Jesus told us in John 14: 1-3, "Let not your heart be troubled: ye believe in God, believe also in Me. In my Father's house are many mansions: if it were not so, I would have told you. I go to prepare a place for you. And if I go and prepare a place for you, I will come again, and receive you unto myself; that where I am, there ye may be also." We have a place that is prepared by God for us. A home where God will dwell with us forever.

It is nice to have a place to belong, Luke tells, in Luke 10:20 that we can have our name recorded in Heaven. In the book of Hebrews 11:16 it states that we are desiring a better country, as did those who have gone on before us, "But now they desire a better country, that is, a heavenly: wherefore God is not ashamed to be called their God: for He hath prepared for them a city." On the subject of longing for a better country, Dan Schaeffer writes in his book *A Better Country Preparing for Heaven,* "There are times here on earth when life is simply wonderful, and we can't imagine leaving it. There are other times when life is so painful it is difficult to bear another day. But even in the best of times, relationships are difficult, circumstances are unpredictable, health is a perpetual struggle, happiness takes wings, and deep down we long for a perfect life without stress and pain. What we're wishing for is what we were made for – the better country, even if we don't recognize it as that. I know for years I didn't recognize my longing as a desire for heaven." (Schaeffer, Dan 2008)

We should not be so attached to this world that it fades our longing for Heaven. We are strangers and pilgrims here on earth, but our citizenship is in Heaven. So many times, we find ourselves wrapped up in things pertaining to this life here on earth that life gets in the way. The hope of the resurrection is that someday we will see the day with no sorrow, no pain, no tears, and no more curse of sin.

The Bible in 1Corinthians 2:9 it tells us that we cannot imagine what Heaven will be like it reads, "But as it is written, eye hath not seen, nor ear heard, neither have entered into the heart of man, the things which God hath prepared for them that love Him." We may not be able to understand or imagine all the wonders of Heaven, but we know that we shall be with our loving Saviour the Lord Jesus Christ.

The power of the resurrection proves to us that we need not fear death, because death does not have the last word. Because of the hope of the resurrection, we can have a home in Heaven.

My prayer is that we all will come to know the power of the resurrection. The power to live changed lives. The power to live victorious lives. The power to live each day surrendered to God's will. The power to know Him and the power of His Resurrection.

Written by Alvin Russell White Jr.

REFERENCE LIST:

Greathouse, M. William. 1958. The Fullness of the Spirit. Kansas City, MO.

Beacon Hill Press of Kansas City

Schaeffer, Dan. 2008. A Better Country Preparing for Heaven.

Grand Rapids, MI. Discovery House

SCRIPTURE REFERENCE LIST:

All Scripture is quoted from the KJV.

Genesis: 1,27; 2:15-17; 3:14-19, 24; 9:5
Exodus: 32:30-32
1Samuel: 12:23
Job: 19:25-26
Psalm: 51:10; 66:18; 139:23-24
Isaiah: 6:3; 11:6; 59:2
Matthew: 1:20; 5:16, 23,24, 25, 38, 39, 45, 46, 47; 6:14, 15; 7:12,13, 14; 28:6, 18,19,20,
Mark: 14:27,31,50; 16:2,3,4
Luke: 5:29; 8:38 - 40; 19:8-9 22:2 - 6; 24-26,32
John: 1:29; 3:16,17; 4:28,29,39; 8:36; 13:1; 14:1,2,3,16; 16:7,13; 17:9,11,13,15,19,24
Acts: 1:8; 2:36; 4:31; 17:2-3
Romans: 5:8,10,12; 6:1-2,7-12,23; 8: 11,22,34; 12:21
1Corinthians: 2:9; 6:14
2Corinthians 3:18; 4:14,16; 5:17
Galatians: 2:20; 5:1,24-25; 6:2

Ephesians: 4:22-23,27; 6:19,20
Philippians: 3:10; 4:13
Colossians: 3:12-13
1Tessalonians: 4:13-18
1Timothy: 2:1
2Timothy: 2:15
Hebrews: 4:14-16; 7:25, 9:11-14,22,25; 11:16
James: 4:7-10; 5:16
1Peter 1:3-5; 2:24; 3:15; 5:7
1John: 1:5; 2:1; 3:1, -3,8,9; 4:4,9-10
Revelation: 21:1-4

Song Reference List:

At Calvary – William R. Newell, 1895

Because He Lives – Gaither, 1971

Dare to be a Daniel – P.P. Bliss, 1873

Glorious Freedom – Haldor Lillenas, 1917

He Abides – Herbert Buffum, 1879

More of This Love – author unknown

Ready – A.C. Palmer, 1845

Savior Like a Shepherd Lead Us – Dorothy Ann Thrupp, 1836

Sweet Hour of Prayer – William Walford, 1845

We Shell See Jesus – Dianne Wilkinson, 1981

Zion's Hill – James A. Crutchfield, 1923

Made in the USA
Middletown, DE
14 January 2024